INDEX

Questions and Answers About Saints

What is a saint?

A saint is a special friend of God who lived a holy life and now lives with God in heaven.

Why do we see pictures or statues of saints? Why are some saints famous?

The Church calls some holy people "saints." The Church wants us to know their stories because saints did everything for God. Many saints cared for the sick with great love. Some were best at teaching about Jesus and God's love. Some were very brave and even died for their belief in God. Some saints were so generous. They sold all their things and gave the money to the poor. Saints are heroes of our faith.

How do we honor saints?

Schools, churches, streets, and cities are often named after saints. Catholics are also given a saint's name at baptism. Saints are honored in pictures, on statues, or on medals. Saints also have feast days to honor them. On feast days of the saints, we remember their stories and ask for their help.

When did the saints live?

Many saints lived long ago. Some, like St. Peter, were among the first friends of Jesus. There were saints – holy men, women, and children – in every century. Some saints lived in modern times.

Where did the saints live?

Saints have served God all around the world. The first saints lived in the land where Jesus lived. Later, Christians and Christian saints lived and served in every nation. There are saints from your country, too.

How can saints help us?

In heaven, saints ask God to help and bless us. We can also ask saints to help us to pray. The saints are happy to help us. They love God and know that we are God's sons and daughters.

St. Joseph

St. Joseph was a good carpenter. When Joseph first learned that Mary was having a baby, he was sad and confused. Joseph and Mary were not yet married. An angel, however, told Joseph in a dream that Mary's baby was the Son of God. Joseph was a man of faith in God. He believed the angel and became Mary's husband.

Before Jesus was born, Mary and Joseph had to travel to Bethlehem so that they could put their names on the ruler's list and be counted. Joseph looked for a place to stay. He found only a stable, a small barn for animals. It was not fancy, but it was warm and safe. Baby Jesus was born there. Joseph took good care of Jesus and Mary.

The family lived in the small town of Nazareth. Joseph taught Jesus his Jewish prayers and many other things. For example, Joseph taught Jesus his trade of carpentry (making things out of wood). Jesus loved his foster father, Joseph.

Activities:

1. Complete the roof on the stable to protect Baby Jesus and his family from the weather.

2. Color the scene of the first Christmas in Bethlehem.

St. Peter

Peter's real name was Simon. In his Judean town near the Sea of Galilee, everybody knew "Simon the fisherman." Simon was married, had a family, and was a good Jew.

When Simon first met Jesus, he didn't know that Jesus was the Son of God. Then one day, Jesus asked Simon and his friends to go fishing. After trying to catch fish all night, they complained to Jesus that they hadn't caught any. Jesus then told Simon what to do. Simon obeyed Jesus, and suddenly their nets were overflowing with fish. From that day, Simon believed that Jesus was God's Son.

Jesus had great plans for Simon. He renamed Simon "Peter" or "Rock" because Peter's faith and courage were strong. Peter became the first pope (a special leader) of the Roman Catholic Church. St. Peter is buried in a special area below the altar in St. Peter's Basilica (a special church) in Rome, Italy, where the pope lives.

Activities:

1. Draw many fish in Peter's net.

2. Write the words (in the space provided) Peter might have said when he saw all the fish.

3. Name the present pope. Where does he live?

St. Paul

Paul was known as "Saul" in Tarsus, a city in modern Turkey. Saul made tents and then sold them to make a living. Saul also studied Jewish law and became an expert and a teacher. When Saul heard about the Christians, he was very angry. Christians believed that Jesus was God's Son, and Saul wouldn't believe that. Then one day, Saul was going to Damascus to help arrest Christians. Along the way, a blinding light suddenly shone and forced Saul to fall on the ground. Jesus told Saul to stop hurting Christians. It was then that Saul realized that Jesus was God's Son. Saul began to study and learn about Jesus and was finally baptized a Christian. During the years that followed, Paul traveled to many cities teaching and writing to people about Jesus. Because most of the people he visited were not Jewish, he used his non-Jewish (Gentile) name, "Paul," and is often referred to as the Apostle of the Gentiles.

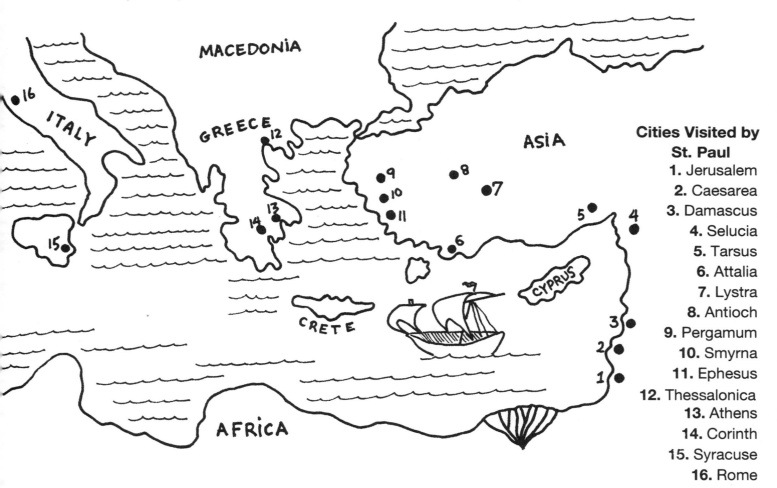

Cities Visited by St. Paul
1. Jerusalem
2. Caesarea
3. Damascus
4. Selucia
5. Tarsus
6. Attalia
7. Lystra
8. Antioch
9. Pergamum
10. Smyrna
11. Ephesus
12. Thessalonica
13. Athens
14. Corinth
15. Syracuse
16. Rome

Activities:

1. Starting with Jerusalem, connect the dots to show the journeys of St. Paul.

2. Read the list of cities Paul visited. Do you recognize any of the names? Share what you know.

3. Color the water blue and the land area beige or tan.

4. Talk about the things St. Paul might have needed to take on his journeys.

St. Valentine

St. Valentine was a priest in Rome a long time ago. In Rome the powerful people believed in many different gods. They prayed to gods for war, healing, sleep, marriage, hunting, and many other things. Valentine knew that there is only one God with three persons — Father, Son, and Holy Spirit. Valentine believed that Jesus, the Son of God, came to earth to show God's great love for each of us. Because Valentine would not pray to the false Roman gods, he was arrested and punished. While in prison, he asked God to heal his jailer's little daughter, who was blind. After the child was healed, the jailer told Valentine that he and his whole family would become Christians. Valentine died for his faith in the one true God on February 14. Christians around the world honor the memory of St. Valentine on February 14 by showing love for others. Cards, candies, flowers, and other special gifts are given to family members and good friends.

Activities:

1. Find twelve large and small valentine hearts hidden in the picture and color them red.

2. Talk about different ways that you can show love to friends and family members.

St. Monica

St. Monica had three children, but she always worried most about her oldest — Augustine. Monica was a Christian, but her husband was not. Monica always prayed hard that her children would be good Christians. As a teenager, Augustine became very wild and selfish. He was a good student but just wouldn't listen to his mother. Day after day, Monica begged Augustine to respect and obey God's laws. Monica never gave up prayer. And just before she died, Augustine changed his sinful ways. He returned to his Christian faith and even started a religious community. He was ordained a priest and after a few years became a bishop in Africa. Augustine said that his life really changed because his mother never stopped praying for him. And God answered her prayers.

Activities:

1. See St. Monica on the beach praying that Augustine would change his ways. Use the code box below to find Monica's message to her son.

2. Use the code box below or make up your own to write a message about God's love to a friend.

A =	B =	D =	E =	G =	H =
I =	N =	O =	P =	S =	Y =

St. Nicholas

Nicholas was a loving and generous bishop in the city of Myra. Nicholas helped the poor people as much as he could. There were many wonderful stories told about the ways Nicholas gave people help and gifts. In one such popular story, Nicholas is said to have met a poor man who had three beautiful daughters. The father was sad. He loved his daughters, but had no money to help them get married. One night, Bishop Nicholas tossed a bag of money into the man's house. The happy man could now help his first daughter get married. Later, Nicholas is said to have tossed two more money bags through a window for the man's other two daughters.

For stories like this, St. Nicholas, the first Santa Claus, became a favorite saint among children. On the night before the feast of St. Nicholas, many children around the world put out their shoes. They hope to find them filled with gifts or treats in the morning.

_____

_____

_____

Activities:

1. Below the present, list the things you could give or share with someone else in need.
   (Don't forget to consider things that only take your time or talent to accomplish, too.)

2. In the open area, draw one or more of the things you listed in the first activity.

3. Tell about your favorite birthday or Christmas gift.

St. Patrick

Life was hard for the young St. Patrick. As a teenager, he was kidnapped and sent as a slave and shepherd to Ireland. On cold, windy green hills, his only companions were sheep! Far from home, Patrick was sad and lonely. Slowly, he learned to pray. Talking to God helped him find joy, peace, and hope. Patrick's faith grew strong.

After six years, Patrick dreamed that God wanted him to escape. He ran away to freedom but later returned to Ireland as a priest and bishop. Patrick wanted to teach the people about God and the life of Jesus. One day he held up a green three-leaf clover. "This little clover," he said with a smile, "can teach us a big lesson about God. See the three leaves?" he asked, as he waived the clover leaf back and forth. "God is three persons — Father, Son, and Holy Spirit." The people understood, and their faith and love of God and Patrick grew.

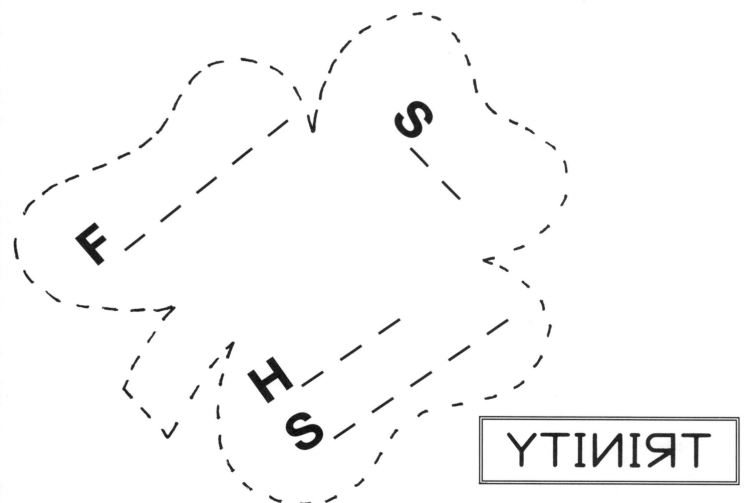

Activities:

1. Connect the lines to form a shamrock and complete the names on each leaf.

2. What one word do we use to refer to the three persons in one God? Check your answer by holding this page in front of a mirror and looking at the letters in the boxed area.

3. Color the shamrock.

St. Benedict

Benedict and his twin sister came from a rich and famous family of Italy. Benedict went to school in Rome. At the time, Rome was the most powerful city in the world, yet Benedict was sad. He had a strong Christian faith and loved God very much, but Benedict saw that most Romans did not. Many, in fact, were selfish and sinful. So Benedict left Rome to look for a quiet and simple place to live and pray. He didn't want a huge house or lots of fancy things. For years Benedict lived in a dark, damp cave. Benedict found it easy to pray there. Many people knew that Benedict was a wise and holy man. Some came to live and pray with him. These followers were called Benedictines. Later, Benedict built large houses of prayer called "monasteries," but he never forgot his quiet cave.

Activities:

1. Tell why St. Benedict lived in a cave.

2. Help St. Benedict find and circle the eleven hidden words carved on the wall of the cave.

3. What are monasteries? Why did St. Benedict build them?

St. Francis of Assisi

The son of a rich merchant, St. Francis became a soldier to find adventure and glory. At twenty, he was captured and became ill in prison. Francis had lots of time to think. He learned that God wanted him to live in a new way. When he was freed, Francis gave all his things back to his father. He began to beg for what he needed. At the same time, Francis saw God's love everywhere. Francis sang about the beauty of the sun, moon, trees, flowers, the rivers and oceans. He said that animals were like our brothers and sisters — all part of God's big family. Once a big wolf attacked people near the village of Gubbio. The people were terrified. Francis went to Gubbio to find the wolf and make peace with him. The The villagers fed and cared for the peaceful wolf until he died.

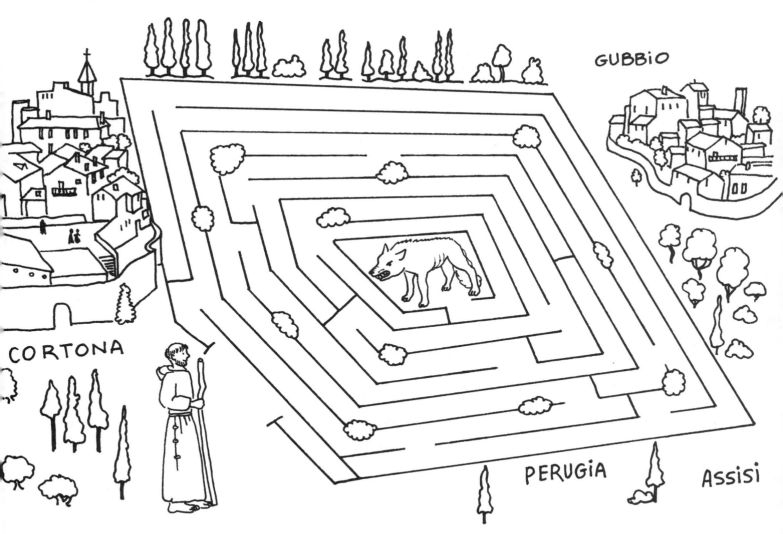

Activities:

1. Draw a line to help St. Francis find the shortest path to reach the wolf.

2. Pretend you are Francis . . . or the wolf of Gubbio. What does Francis say to make peace between "Brother Wolf" and the people of Gubbio? What does the wolf say?

St. Elizabeth

St. Elizabeth was just a girl when she married the future king of Hungary. Ludwig loved his young wife so much and Elizabeth felt the same way about Ludwig. Soon, the royal couple thanked God for three little children. Elizabeth's loving heart reached out to all. Whenever she heard about a hungry family, she took them food from her own kitchen. But not everyone thought that it was a good idea to feed the poor. Some selfish people said that the queen wasted too much money on the needy. One day, Elizabeth had an armload of bread for a poor family. The loaves were hidden under her cloak. When an angry soldier pulled back her cloak, the loaves turned into beautiful roses. God had helped Elizabeth, who helped the poor. When young King Ludwig was killed in a war, his wife and children were thrown out of their home. Elizabeth died at the age of twenty-four while caring for sick people.

Activities:

1. Color the roses in Queen Elizabeth's arms.

2. How did Queen Elizabeth show her love for God?

12

St. Joan of Arc

Arc was such a quiet, little village. Joan was the youngest child of a peasant family. Like most people, she could not read and knew little about the world. The slender, pretty girl, however, knew how to pray and loved God very much. She also loved going to Mass and hearing the priest tell Bible stories. When she was fourteen, Joan sensed that God had a special plan for her — and her country. England had attacked France and was trying to kill the future king, Prince Charles. Joan knew nothing about being a soldier. However, with God's help Joan became a great one and led the soldiers of France to victory over the English. With Joan by his side, Prince Charles was crowned King Charles VII. The following year Joan was wounded and captured. Joan's enemies lied about her and her great love of God. At nineteen, Joan was killed while praying and holding a cross.

1 _____

2 _____

3 _____

4 _____

5 _____

6 _____

7 _____

8 _____

9 _____

10 _____

_____

_____

_____

Activities:

1. Identify and name the numbered items that Joan needed as a soldier.
   Write your answers in the numbered spaces provided.

2. Think of other items Joan might have needed and write them on the extra lines.

13

St. Juan Diego

Nine miles to church was not such a long walk. However, Juan Diego was fifty-five and had aches and pains in his bare feet. Near the top of a hill, he heard some birds chirping. Juan wondered why these wonderful summer sounds could be heard in cold December. A beautiful, shining Aztec lady was smiling at him. She called his name, and Juan went closer. The young woman said she was Mary, the mother of God's son, Jesus. She wanted to show Juan's people how much God loved them.

The bishop would not believe Juan's story about Mary's visit. Two days later, Juan carried roses in his cloak from Mary's hill to show the bishop. This would be proof, because roses didn't ever grow in that area during December. Also, inside Juan's cloak was a beautiful picture of Our Lady of Guadalupe. Juan smiled in surprise. What a special and wonderful gift from the lady on the hill.

Prayer to Our Lady of Guadalupe

Mary, you are *Our Lady of Guadalupe.* Long ago, you left a beautiful picture of yourself on Juan Diego's cloak. Juan shared this picture with the world. You are a loving mother for all, but I know that the needs of children are your special concern. Protect me and all children today. Help me to follow your son, Jesus, in what I say and do. Amen.

Color Key

Radiant lines (—) = yellow
Mary's mantle = blue
Mary's robe = pink
Moon = black
Angel = red
Angel wings = orange and red
Roses = red, pink, orange, and yellow
Juan's cloak = light blue

Activities:

1. Using the colors suggested above, color the picture of *Our Lady of Guadalupe.*

2. Say the prayer to *Our Lady of Guadalupe.*

St. Rose of Lima

"Rose" was a better name for the girl named "Isabel." As a baby, Isabel was so pretty and pink. Many people in Lima, Peru, called her "Rose" even before her family used the nickname. As a young woman, Rose also had a beautiful spirit and heart. She loved God so much that she wanted to spend her time praying and helping others.

To make a living, Rose grew vegetables, flowers, and herbs. She sold them at the farmer's market in the city. Rose also earned money with her embroidery, a special kind of sewing. Every day Rose visited sick and poor people in the big city of Lima. She had learned how to make medicines from herbs. The people loved their beautiful *Rose.* She was as good as she was beautiful.

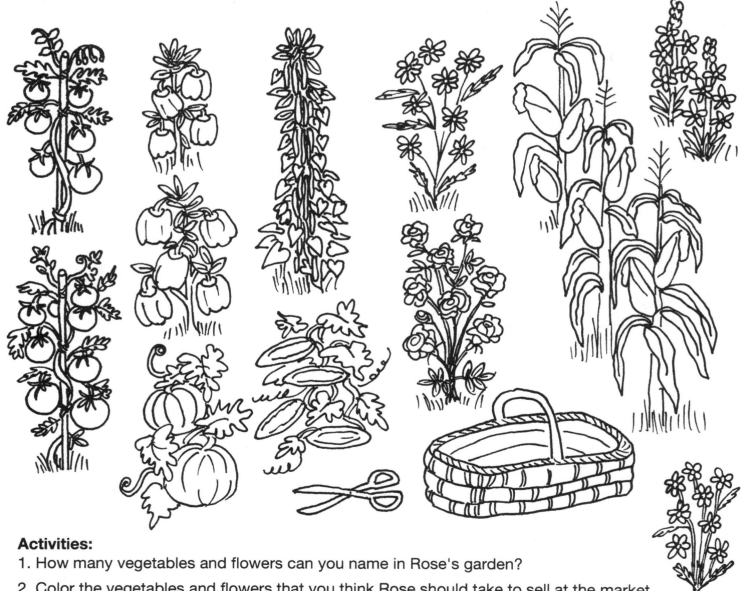

Activities:

1. How many vegetables and flowers can you name in Rose's garden?

2. Color the vegetables and flowers that you think Rose should take to sell at the market.

3. Discuss: Have you ever helped grow flowers, fruits, or vegetables to share with others?

St. Martin de Porres

Martin was the son of a black woman and a Spanish knight. Martin's father didn't like the black skin that God gave Martin and his younger sister. That hurt Martin's feelings. He learned, however, that God the Father loved him just as he was. And Martin, in turn, loved God with all his heart. Martin was smart, too, and became a barber, physician, and a Dominican brother. Brother Martin soon became a very popular man in Lima, Peru. Martin would bandage wounds, give medicines, and pray for everyone he met. Martin collected money from rich people to help build a hospital and orphanage. He also ran a shelter for stray animals. "They are God's creatures," he explained. Martin even made friends with some mice and coaxed them outside the chapel, where he fed them. The naughty mice had chewed on the altar clothes and Mass vestments! When Martin was dying, the ruler of Peru came to ask for his blessing. Everyone in Lima soon missed Brother Martin.

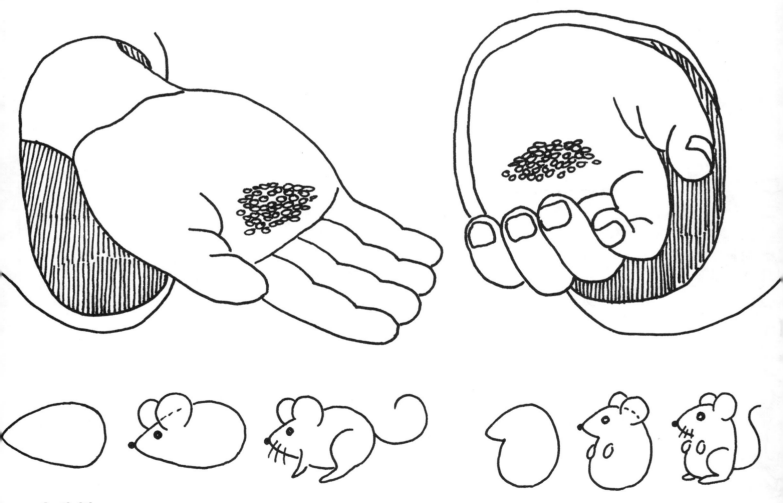

Activities:

1. Draw and color two mice among the bread crumbs Martin is holding in his hands.
   Use the guidelines provided above if you need help drawing the mice.

2. Discuss: What might have Martin said to the "dinner guests" that you drew in his hands?

Bl. Kateri Tekakwitha

Tekakwitha, a shy Mohawk Indian girl, didn't remember much about her parents. They had died from a disease when she was very young. She wondered why they named her "Tekakwitha." The word meant "she puts things in order." Tekakwitha lived with her uncle in Ossernenon, a village in an area that is now part of the city of New York. Winters were cold, and the Indians were often hungry. Indian tribes often attacked each other. Warriors killed or kidnapped some people and burned the bark-covered homes of others. When Tekakwitha heard about Jesus from French priests, she wanted to be a Christian. Jesus taught a new way to live. Living like Jesus would put her life in order, Tekakwitha told herself. The girl's family, however, was angry. They didn't trust the white priests or their teachings. At twenty, Tekakwitha was secretly baptized. She hid her cross and rosary. One night, she ran away to Caughnawaga, a Christian village in Canada. There Tekakwitha was so happy. She could pray without hiding.

Note: Blessed Kateri has completed the second of three stages in the Church's formal process of declaring someone a saint. The final stage, called "canonization," should be completed shortly.

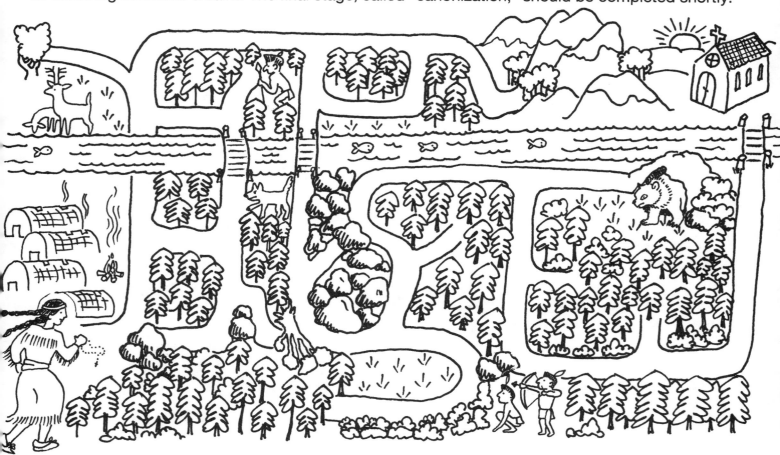

Activities:

1. With your finger, find the best trail for Tekakwitha to take to get to the village of Caughnawaga.
2. Mark the trail with little crosses that will lead Tekakwitha to freedom and to other Christians.
3. Draw a large cross near the little church in Caughnawaga, Canada.

Bl. Junípero Serra

Each day, Father Junípero thanked God for many things. California's beautiful skies and ocean reminded him of the island near Spain where he was born. This happy, cheerful Franciscan priest also was pleased that many Indians were now Christians. Junípero and other missionaries were busy teaching the people about Jesus. The people loved to hear Gospel stories, especially those about Jesus healing the sick. The Franciscans also were teaching the Indians about farming, raising cattle, and building strong, new houses. Junípero himself was a fine carpenter. He helped design and build the twenty-one mission churches located up and down the California coast. The first mission was built at San Diego in 1769. The missions were named after saints. Each mission was a day's walk from the next mission. The humble Padre Junípero would not take credit for building these beautiful missions. God just wanted people to know God, the padre said. And God wanted to welcome everyone into his new house.

Note: Blessed Junípero has completed the second of three stages in the Church's formal process of declaring someone a saint. The final stage, called "canonization," should be completed shortly.

Activities:

1. Connect the dots to complete the drawing.

2. Color the picture of Padre Junípero's mission.

18

St. Elizabeth Ann Seton

There was so much to teach the girls! Some days, "Mother" Elizabeth Ann Seton didn't know where to begin. Her little school was the first Catholic grade school in Maryland and in the United States! But it wasn't famous or fancy. In the winter, snow drifted down through the many cracks in the roof. The children had few school supplies and books. But Mother Seton, a widow and mother of five, loved to teach. Her own daughters sat among white, Native American, and black girls on the school benches. The girls were eager to read, write, and do math problems. Mother Seton, a new Catholic herself, talked about her faith. She also read Bible stories and gave the girls puzzles that taught Bible verses. Mother Seton was so thankful that God was blessing her work. Other women were joining her to form a new order of sisters in the United States called the "Daughters of Charity." Like her students, these sisters loved calling Elizabeth "Mother Seton."

Jesus said,

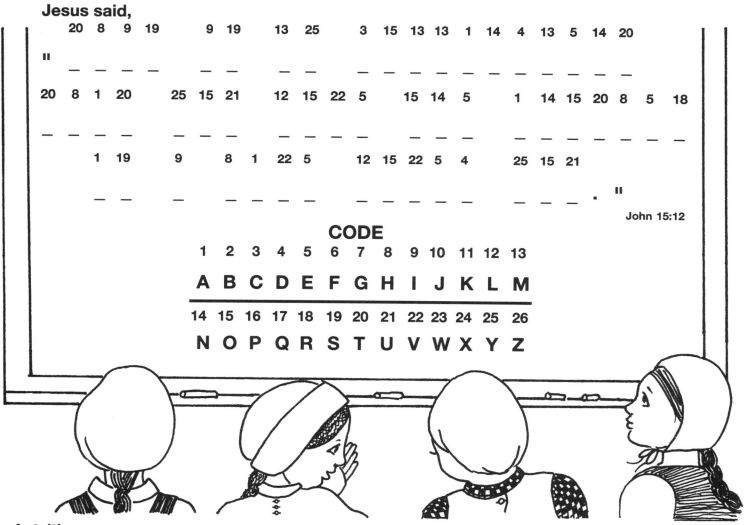

John 15:12

CODE

1	2	3	4	5	6	7	8	9	10	11	12	13
A	B	C	D	E	F	G	H	I	J	K	L	M

14	15	16	17	18	19	20	21	22	23	24	25	26
N	O	P	Q	R	S	T	U	V	W	X	Y	Z

Actvities:
1. Use the code box to unscramble this Bible verse and write it on the lines provided.
2. Learn this Bible verse by heart — just as Mother Seton's students would have.

19

St. John Bosco

John Bosco knew how hard a boy's life can be. He was only two years old when his father died. John's family was already poor. Now, John's mother, Margaret, had to care for three little boys all by herself. As a schoolboy, John often went to the circus and carnivals to learn magic tricks and stunts. He gave his own little shows to raise money for his family. John surely loved his family, but he also loved God.

When he became a priest, John saw many poor and homeless boys running through the streets. Father John made arrangements to provide them a loving home and school. To make his sad boys laugh, Father would perform magic tricks or stand on his hands. To help him in his work with the boys, Father John organized an order of priests called the Society of St. Francis de Sales (Salesians). Later he founded an order of religious sisters to help him care for poor and neglected girls. Because Jesus was gentle and patient, Father John always treated his children with loving kindness.

Activities

1. Draw and color three or four items that Father John might have juggled. Tell about your drawing.

2. Discuss who helped Father John take care of homeless boys and girls.

St. Bernadette

On a cold February day, Bernadette and two other girls went to find firewood. At fourteen, Bernadette was the oldest, but she was small and sickly. She coughed and coughed as she pulled off her socks and shoes to cross an icy stream. Suddenly, Bernadette saw a beautiful lady. The lady, dressed in a lovely white gown, seemed to be standing on air in a little cave called a grotto. Bernadette was scared and reached for the rosary in her pocket. The lady said nothing but held her own rosary as Bernadette prayed.

The lady appeared eighteen times to Bernadette alone. During one appearance, the lady told Bernadette that she was the Virgin Mary, the Mother of God's son, Jesus. She wanted Lourdes to be a place where people asked God for healing. The Virgin Mary asked people to pray and be good. Bernadette became a religious sister and spent the rest of her short life doing what Mary had asked.

Activities

1. Color the scene. Mary's gown should be white, her sash blue, and the roses at her feet yellow.

2. Say a "Hail Mary." It is the prayer that Bernadette often prayed with "Our Lady of Lourdes."

Hail Mary, full of grace, the Lord is with you. Blessed are you among women and blessed is the fruit of your womb, Jesus. Holy Mary, Mother of God, pray for us sinners, now and at the hour of our death. Amen.

St. Katharine Drexel

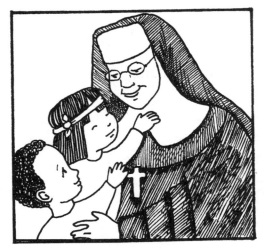

The floors shined when Mother Katharine scrubbed them. She also cooked, washed dishes, and folded laundry as well as any nun in the house. Pretty good for a millionaire's daughter! She grew up in a house with dozens of servants. But the rich Drexel family also was loving and generous. Katharine's parents invited poor people to dinner twice a week. It was big news in Philadelphia when young Katharine gave up a fancy lifestyle to become a religious sister. Katharine wanted to serve God by serving Native and black Americans, who were then often poor and uneducated. Katharine used her family's fortune – more than $20 million – to start schools, missions, and Xavier University for blacks in New Orleans. In spite of hard and dedicated work, Mother Katharine was always cheerful.

How to Share a Million Dollars

Activities

1. Color the million dollar bill green.

2. Imagine that St. Katharine Drexel gave you one million dollars to share with needy people — discuss programs and ways you might spend money to help them.

3. Discuss ways you can help others without spending money.

22

St. Thérèse of Lisieux

Saint Thérèse was the baby of her family. The youngest of nine children, Thérèse was four when her mother died. She became sad and serious. Her big sisters became little mothers for her. When two of her older sisters became nuns, Thérèse followed their example. In the Carmelite convent, Sister Thérèse of the Child Jesus had a new way to serve God. The young nun would do boring or messy jobs with a big smile. When other sisters were annoying or unkind, Thérèse never got mad. She tried to make the best of things. Thérèse always talked to God about the hard moments — and the happy moments — of her day. Thérèse called this "the little way" to God. Everyone can follow "the little way." God loves our little steps toward him, Thérèse said. She was asked to write about her childhood and her life in the convent. Titled "The Story of a Soul," her book became a famous spiritual autobiography. Thérèse died at the age of twenty-four from tuberculosis. People often refer to her as "The Little Flower."

Henry's Day and "The Little Way"

1.
Henry wakes up to find that it's raining and he won't be able to play outside.

2.
In school, Henry's friend Mike purposely pushes Henry's books off his desk.

3.
Henry is happy to get an "A" on a big test.

4.
At home, Henry's little brother breaks Henry's favorite remote-control car.

5.
Henry's mom asks him to set the dinner table even though it's his sister's job.

Activities

1. Read through the various events in Henry's day. Then talk about what Henry might do or say in each situation.

2. Then describe how Henry could please God (and make the best of things) by what he says or does in each of the five events.

3. Talk about how you can do little things for others to please God.

23

St. Edith Stein

As a teenager, Edith Stein didn't believe in God. She thought that prayer was a silly waste of time. The Stein family had been faithful Jews for centuries. Edith's lack of faith made her mother very sad. Mrs Stein prayed that Edith would find God again. All the Steins were proud of Edith's great work in school. Edith won scholarships and became a university teacher. When Edith met a young Catholic couple, she became interested in Catholicism. As war began in Germany, God seemed very real to Edith. She became a Catholic and a nun. She believed that God is the Father of all people and all faiths. Edith still said Jewish prayers in Hebrew and was proud of being a Jew. She reminded people that Jesus was a Jew. Because she was Jewish, Edith was killed in a prison camp during World War II.

Activities

1. Color all the pieces of the puzzle containing a large black dot. You will discover a Hebrew word and its meaning. It is a word that is traditionally used both as a greeting and a farewell.

2. Use this word today with a friend or someone in your family.

24